A
I
A

Nation-Building in Yugoslavia:
A Study of Political Integration and Attitudinal Consensus

GARY K. BERTSCH
University of Georgia

SAGE PUBLICATIONS / Beverly Hills / London

For information address:

SAGE PUBLICATIONS, INC.
275 South Beverly Drive
Beverly Hills, California 90212

SAGE PUBLICATIONS LTD
St George's House / 44 Hatton Garden
London E C 1

International Standard Book Number 0-8039-0140-2

Library of Congress Catalog Card No. 70-172475

FIRST PRINTING

CONTENTS

LIST OF TABLES AND FIGURES

Nation-Building in Yugoslavia:
A Study of Political Integration and Attitudinal Consensus

GARY K. BERTSCH
University of Georgia

INTRODUCTION

The prime objective of this analysis is to provide a greater awareness and understanding of the "nation-building" process in the Yugoslav socio-political system.[1] Two separate components of nation-building will be considered in this analysis. The first, *political integration,* refers to a component reflecting values and attitudes closely related to the development of "community" among a population of diverse social groupings attempting to form a greater multinational, political entity. The second, *attitudinal consensus,* refers to a component reflecting the extent of similarity, or, conversely, dissimilarity in attitudes and values characterizing the various social aggregates composing a larger political entity. It is assumed that the extent of community (i.e., political integration) and the similarity of attitudes (i.e., attitudinal consensus) among social aggregates within Yugoslav society can be viewed and assessed at one point in time as manifest within the system of beliefs and values of the citizenry making up that society.

AUTHOR'S NOTE: The author would like to acknowledge that the data used in this investigation were collected in 1967 by the Centar za Istrazivanje Javnog Mnenja (Center for the Research of Public Opinion) in Belgrade, Yugoslavia. The survey work was sponsored and directed by Professor M. George Zaninovich, Department of Political Science, University of Oregon, and was carried out to provide the survey data required for his study entitled "Value Change in Yugoslav Society." *The author is indebted to Provessor Zaninovich for use of the survey data.*

Kark Deutsch in the introductory chapter of *Nation-Building* (Deutsch and Foltz, 1963: 6) asks, "Just what do we mean when we say that . . . (a) social and political attachment to a small ethnic, cultural, or linguistic group has been overcome in the process of national integration?" He subsequently answers that question (Deutsch and Foltz 1963: 7-8; italics added):

> Open or latent resistance to political amalgamation into a common national state; minimal integration to the point of passive compliance with the orders of such an amalgamated government; deeper political integration to the point of active support for such a common state but with continuing ethnic or cultural group cohesion and diversity; and finally, *the coincidence of political amalgamation and integration with the assimilation of all groups to a common culture*—these could be the main stages on the way from tribes to nation. However, since a nation is not an animal or vegetable organism, its evolution need not go through any fixed sequence of these steps.

The sequence that any developing social system evolves through is usually uncharted and often complex. This has been particularly true in the case of the Yugoslav. The following analysis will address itself to what Deutsch seems to refer to as one of the latter stages of the developmental sequence ("political amalgamation and integration with the assimilation of all groups to a common culture"), a stage which is acknowledged by most developmental theorists to be of particular revelance to the nation-building process.

THEORETICAL FRAMEWORK

Research on the components of political integration and attitudinal consensus must take into account the fact that different populations within a dynamic, developing social system may become increasingly integrated or similar at different rates of speed due to the particular nature of the group. Therefore, it may be feasible to conceive of particular populations as holding different positions along the "roads" or processes leading to higher levels of integration and societal consensus. One population may be judged as highly integrated; another may be judged as currently occupying a rather untenable position verging on integration, or in other words, may be occupying what could be referred to as the "threshold" level; while yet another may be assessed as considerably less integrated than other populations. The same would also be true for what can be identified as the separate component of attitudinal consensus.

In view of this assumption and through the use of survey research data, this investigation has attempted to assess where a number of Yugoslav populations were as of 1967 in reference to the construction of the Yugoslav socialist community.

Political integration, as used in this investigation, will refer to a number of attitudinal dimensions. When viewing the "politically integrated" individual, the dimensions and related attidudinal statements can be viewed as follows:

(1) a deemphasis of particularistic elements within the Yugoslav context such as national-regional dialect

(2) a deemphasis of the role of nationality (i.e., Croat, Serb, and the like) within the country

(3) a willingness to resettle, reside, and work in *any* national-regional area within the Yugoslav state if the need for work so requires

(4) an orientation attaching importance to and supporting Yugoslav state celebrations

(5) a feeling of faith and confidence in the diverse Yugoslav peoples

(6) a willingness to converse with individuals of different thoughts and backgrounds thereby exhibiting a tolerance for the diversity present in Yugoslav society

Each of these dimensions is represented by a value statement drawn from the survey instrument.[2] The individual statements, in turn, will be used to construct an index representing the political integration component.[3]

Attitudinal consensus, on the other hand, refers to the degree of attitudinal similarity among defined populations of the larger Yugoslav sample on an extensive number of evaluative statements drawn from the survey instrument.[4]

Political integration is conceived, therefore, as a multidimensional concept. Hence, it is possible for a particular population to be highly integrated on one dimension (e.g., a deemphasis of the importance of nationality) while being considerably less integrated on another dimension (e.g., an absence of support for Yugoslav state celebrations). As a result, it is necessary to assess the various populations on *each* of the separate dimensions in order to make an objective assessment of overall integration levels.

It is also necessary to consider a multiplicity of dimensions when considering attitudinal consensus. For example, a population within Yugoslavia could hold an attitudinal configuration very similar to the countrywide sample on one issue while holding a configuration very different from the larger sample on another. In order to make an overall assessment of a populations's attitudinal posture, it is therefore necessary to consider its position on a number of different dimensions.

By way of summary, then, political integration asks how a specific population is attitudinally oriented toward value questions related to the construction of a multinational Yugoslav state. While, contrastingly, cultural convergence asks where a population stands in relation to the countrywide sample on an extensive number of evaluative statements. The difference between the two concepts, and also their close theoretical relationship, can be best illustrated in a fourfold typology (see Figure 1).

		Attitudinal Consensus	
		High	Low
Political Integration	High	(a)	(b)
	Low	(c)	(d)

Figure 1. TYPOLOGY ILLUSTRATING POSSIBLE RANKINGS ON THE INTEGRATION AND CONSENSUS COMPONENTS

Conceivably, any population within Yugoslav society could rank in one of these four classifications. That is, specific populations could be assessed as:

(a) high in terms of political integration and high in terms of attitudinal consensus

(b) high in terms of political integration and low in terms of attitudinal consensus

(c) low in terms of political integration and high in terms of attitudinal consensus

(d) low in terms of political integration and low in terms of attitudinal consensus

Therefore, it is theoretically possible for any population to possess attitudes highly conducive to the establishment of a multinational community, and also possess a system of beliefs very similar to an average expression of the Yugoslav peoples; i.e., classification (a); or conversely, possess attitudes not particularly conducive to the establishment of a multinational community, and a system of beliefs very dissimilar from an average expression of the Yugoslav peoples; i.e., classification (d); or any combination of the above; i.e., (b) or (c). Classification (b) implies that a particular Yugoslav population could respond favorably to the attitudinal preconditions engendering the evolution of the multinational state, and at the same time, cling to its attitudinal divergencies or dissimilarities. For example, one might speculate that this combination could be represented by a culturally diverged nationality inhabiting a geographical area relatively close to the Yugoslav political center (Belgrade). Classification (d) implies that a population may reflect the attitudinal preconditions favorable for the multinational state and at the same time be characterized by belief systems very similar to an average expression of the Yugoslav peoples. One might speculate that this combination could be represented by a population geographically removed from the vital centers of Yugoslav politics but culturally tied to the traditions and attitudes representative of the average Yugoslav expression. In other words, analysis of the data may reveal that there are particular populations reflecting each classification in the fourfold typology.

The foregoing discussion is based upon the obvious assumption that the building of a multinational state in Yugoslavia cannot be considered apart from Yugoslav political culture. Verba (Pye and Verba, 1965: 513) notes that, "the political culture of a society consists of the system of empirical beliefs, expressive symbols and values which defines the situation in which political action takes place. It provides a subjective orientation to politics." The nature of such beliefs and consensus upon them within specific Yugoslav populations are not variables whose values are to be assumed, but rather to be investigated systematically and empirically in the following analysis.

Consideration of integration and value consensus, or of political culture in general, presupposes in turn that these phenomena will have some determinable effect upon the functioning of the political system. That is, what difference does it make to the development of the Yugoslav state that a number of populations within the system are characterized by a very low level of political integration and also are very dissimilar from the larger Yugoslav political culture? The typical social engineer would maintain, and reasonably so, that the presence of a politically integrated and assimilated belief system among different populations permits political action to occur in a manner encouraging compatability and predictability within any sociopolitical unit. For example, Claude Ake, (1967: 3-4; italics added) contends that:

> The political system is integrated to the extent that groups and individual actors within groups develop in the course of political

interaction a pool of commonly accepted norms regarding political behavior and a commitment to political behavior patterns legitimized by such norms. Commitment to these norms channels the flow of exchanges (outputs and inputs, actions and reactions, expectations and responses) among interacting political actors. In effect, it gives *coherence and predictability* to political life.

We should also note that the relationships between higher levels of political integration and attitudinal similarity on the one hand, and higher levels of political pacification, compliance, and stability within present-day Yugoslavia could be attributed to at least some minimal level of integration and consensus within that society. It seems reasonable to maintain, however, that some populations may be lagging in regard to further integration and convergence. Therefore, in order to examine the particular postures reflected by different segments of the society, one must consider the particular beliefs and values held by the defined populations inhabiting the present-day social system.

POPULATIONS

In order to identify the various populations for analysis, the broader Yugoslav sample will be divided according to two different criteria: first, culture-region, and somewhat later, nationality. The reason for using both criteria in the Yugoslav context is obvious due to the importance of both geography and nationality in the country. In other words, it shall be necessary to view the integration and consensus components for all of the inhabitants of one culture-region (e.g., Bosnia-Hercegovina) regardless of nationality (relatively equal representations of Serbs, Croats, and Moslems in Bosnia-Hercegovina) as well as for all those who identify with a particular nationality irrespective of the area of inhabitance (e.g., a considerable representation of Serbs will be found in areas outside of Serbia). According to the first criteria, we are saying that one's culture-region may be of importance, and in the second, we are attaching importance to one's nationality.

When defining the broader sample of 1,186 respondents according to culture-region, it yields populations drawn from the following areas: Serbia Proper with its predominant Serb nationality composition and Orthodox religious affiliation (n = 251); Croatia-Slavonia, with its predominant Croat nationality and Catholic religious affiliation (n = 203); Slovenia, with its concentration of the Slovene nationality and Catholicism (n = 153); Adriatic Coastal with its predominant Croat composition in the north and somewhat more heterogenous composition in the central and southern areas (n = 138); Bosnia-Hercegovina, with its mix of Serb and

Croat nationalities and heterogeneous religious environment (n = 146); and Macedonia, with its concentration of Macedonians, and Albanian and Turk minorities (n = 148). In addition, the following three more unique culture-regions are represented: Montenegro (n = 46), Vojvodina (n = 50), and Kosmet (n = 51) (see Table 1 for figures on the culture-region populations according to the latest census figures and the survey sample). Montenegro was selected because of its homogeneous and largely isolated Montenegrin population; the autonomous region of Vojvodina because of its heterogeneous nationality composition and large Hungarian minority (approximately one-fourth of the population); and the autonomous region of Kosmet because of its predominant Albanian composition.

When dividing the countrywide sample on the basis of national identification, the following populations are produced: Serb (n = 362), Croat (n = 314), Slovene (n = 157), Macedonian (n = 137), Moslem [Slavic] (n = 51), Montenegrin (n = 80), Hungarian (n = 15), Yugoslav (n = 37), Albanian (n = 29) (See Table 2 for the figures and the survey sample). As illustrated in Tables 1 and 2, the survey distribution of the populations defined according to both culture-region and nationality compares closely with the census distribution.

Due to the stratified sampling procedures used in selecting interviewees, relatively the same occupational and educational groupings were selected from each culture-region and nationality grouping. In effect, occupational and educational characteristics have been controlled across regions and nationalities. The value of this sampling procedure for purposes of this study is that the culture-region variable reflects a relatively pure indicator of orientations emanating from cultural-regional influences rather than individual social characteristics since the respondents from each culture-region were characterized basically by the same socioeconomic levels. The same applies, of course, to nationality.

MEASUREMENT TECHNIQUES

In order to permit measurement of the political integration variable, the six evaluative statements listed in Appendix A, Inventory I were selected from a list of 38 statements included in an extensive survey questionnaire administered to the total sample of 1,186 interviewees in Yugoslavia. Mean response scores on each of the six statements were calculated separately for the entire sample and for each of the smaller defined populations within the larger sample. In other words, the individual responses were aggregated to yield a value for the overall sample and for each of the smaller populations. The mean score of a particular population on each statement was then compared to the mean score for the entire sample on

TABLE 1

DISTRIBUTION OF YUGOSLAV POPULATIONS ACCORDING TO CENSUS AND SURVEY BY CULTURE-REGION

Yugoslav Culture Regions	Percentage of Total Population	Number of Total Population	Percentage of Total Sample	Number of Total Sample
Serbia Proper	26.0	4,823,276	21.3	251
Croatia-Slavonia	22.4[a]	4,159,696[a]	16.8	203
Adriatic Coastal	11.6		11.6	138
Slovenia	8.6	1,591,507	12.9	153
Bosnia-Hercegovina	17.7	3,277,935	12.4	146
Macedonia	7.6	1,406,003	12.5	148
Montenegro	2.5	471,894	3.9	46
Vojvodina	10.0	1,854,965	4.3	50
Kosmet	5.2	963,988	4.3	51
Total	100.0	18,549,264	100.0	1,186

SOURCE: Population census figures taken from *Popis Stanovnistva*, 1961, Volume VI.

a. For census purposes, the Croatia-Slavonia and Adriatic Coastal populations are combined.

TABLE 2

DISTRIBUTION OF YUGOSLAV POPULATIONS ACCORDING TO CENSUS AND SURVEY SAMPLE BY NATIONALITY

Yugoslav Nationalities	Percentage of Total Population	Number of Total Population	Percentage of Total Sample	Number of Total Sample
Serb	42.1	7,906,209	30.5	362
Croat	23.1	4,293,852	26.5	314
Slovene	8.6	1,589,176	13.2	157
Macedonian	5.6	1,045,529	11.5	137
Muslimani (Slavic Moslem)	5.2	972,953	4.3	51
Montenegrin	2.8	513,833	6.7	80
Hungarian	2.7	504,368	1.3	15
Yugoslav	1.7	317,125	3.1	37
Albanian	4.9	914,760	2.4	29
Others or unknown	3.3	591,459	.5	4
Total	100.0	18,549,264	100.0	1,186

SOURCE: Population census figures taken from *Popis Stanovnista*, 1961, Volume VI.

the respective statements. If the defined population responded in what was determined to be a "more integrated" manner than did the entire Yugoslav population, it received a score of +1 or +2 depending on how much more integrated its response was than the response of the larger population. If the defined population responded in a "less integrated" manner than did the larger population, it received a score of −1 or −2.[5] The difference between a +1 and +2 score (or −1 and −2) was based upon the distance of a population's mean score away from the larger sample's score as measured by a fraction of standard deviation units. The sum of plus and minus scores on all statements was then used to establish a population's ranking on the Political Integration Index.[6]

Seventeen evaluative statements were selected for the purpose of constructing an index of attitudinal consensus. This index purports to establish levels of a population's similarity to the mean Yugoslav expression on different issues relevant to the Yugoslav sociopolitical scene. In effect, an attempt has been made to arrive at an empirical basis or mean expression of some of the elements defining Yugoslav political culture. The selected method allowed empirical analysis on each statement concerning how far or how close a particular population was to the mean Yugoslav orientation. Again, a population's score on each statement contributed equally to its overall ranking on the Attitudinal Consensus Index.

Specifically, mean scores were calculated on each of the seventeen statements in the index for the entire Yugoslav sample, and for each of the defined populations within the larger sample. The mean score of a particular population on each statement was then compared to the mean score of the entire sample in order to determine how similar the population's aggregate response was to the average Yugoslav response. If the population's response fell within a predetermined distance of that of the entire sample (i.e., was assessed as being "similar" on that orientation), as measured again by a fraction of standard deviation units, the population received a score of +1.[7] If it fell outside this standard deviation unit (i.e., was assessed as being "dissimilar"), it received −1. The difference between plus and minus scores on each of the seventeen statements was then used to establish a population's ranking on the Attitudinal Consensus Index.[8]

Three basic statistical measures were used in the investigation. A measure of typicality, the arithmetic mean, was used to establish a population's "typical" orientation on each evaluative statement in both the consensus and integration indices. The standard deviation was used to establish a base point for purposes of assessing divergencies of particular populations from the Yugoslav mean. For purposes of more intensive attitudinal analysis, an ordinal measure of consensus—the Leik consensus score—was used to assess the solidarity or similarity of specific orientations within the different populations (for a discussion of this measure, see Leik, 1966: 85-90).

POLITICAL INTEGRATION

A historical consideration of the South Slavic peoples is particularly important when attempting to understand why specific populations within the country rank as they do in reference to the political integration component. For example, it would be useful to consider the effect of the historical fact that Slovene national consciousness has been centuries in developing whereas the development of a Macedonian national consciousness within the Yugoslav context is largely a post-World War II phenomenon. What effect might this fact have upon Slovene and Macedonian postures on the Political Integration Index? Unfortunately, in an essay of this length, the ramifications and implications of the rich South Slavic past cannot be investigated in such depth. All that is attempted in this analysis is the development of a classification of Yugoslav populations, and perhaps with luck, a presentation of rather general explanations of what appear to be past and present influences upon existing levels of political integration within particular populations. It is the author's contention that before we can explain why certain Yugoslav nations behave as they do, we need a more objective idea of where they stand.

The very idea of Yugoslav integration is problematical when considering the diversity present in that infinitely complex country. Suffice it to say that ever since the Yugoslavs entered the Balkan lands in the sixth and seventh centuries, the conditions have been such to encourage divisiveness rather than unity. Geographical, political, cultural, economic, and social factors have all tended to divide the South Slavs along a multiplicity of chaotic, but often overlapping, lines. Furthermore, the presence of Austrian, Hungarian, Italian, German, and Turkish overlords invariably created further divisions within the Balkan lands due to their well-known policies of divide and rule. Kerner (1949: 33) remarks that, "It is therefore nothing short of miraculous that the movement for unification was achieved as early as 1918." But although these groups united to form a multinational Yugoslav state at that time, this so-called "union" between disparate partners proved to be more of a basis for ethnoreligious conflict than cooperation during the interwar period. The troublesome union was soon to be dissolved at the hands of the Axis occupiers. Hoffman and Neal (1962: 65) comment in the following manner on the interwar years and what followed:

Between the two World Wars, Yugoslavia was a state but never really a nation. Now, two decades after its establishment, the state vanished. Created by one war, it was destroyed by another. The same was soon, however, to give birth to a new Yugoslavia, very different from its predecessor, yet in many ways much the same.

Yugoslavia's land suffered tragically during the second world war. Its cities were ravaged and its material and human resources wasted. But out of this war a new Yugoslavia was founded, leading one observer to comment:

> Out of these tragic wartime experiences developed what might be termed a partisan myth of solidarity. Given a reality by the passion and suffering of battle, this myth not only served to bind together the leaders of the communist movement, but also helped to solidify the lower echelon, noncommunist rank and file behind a common "Yugoslav" cause [Zaninovich, 1968: 45].

But this is not to say that the Tito-led partisan forces were to return from battle with a homogeneous citizenry and a fully unified state, for the system was still not without its problems. The ethnic situation and other prewar disintegrative tendencies remained, leading the new Communist regime to copy the federal system of the Soviet Union in pattern and operation. The Titoist regime's policy since 1945, however, has been considerably more flexible than the Soviet and has attempted to allow territorial and national autonomy, but concomitantly, to retain some measure of overall control at the center. Consequently, a series of changes between regional autonomy and centralization have occurred over this 25-year period. First, decentralization to satisfy the more particularistic regional elements was followed; then centralization, to achieve a country-wide commitment, and another turn toward greater decentralization. The series of changes is still in flux and no equilibrium is in sight (for a discussion of the postwar nationality question and policy changes, see Shoup, 1968: 184-226). It should be noted that it is within this context, and resulting tendencies for nationalism, disunity, and disintegration, that political integration will be considered.[9]

In the following section, then, populations will be considered in reference to the Political Integration Index as defined first according to culture-region, and, second, according to nationality.

CULTURE-REGION

The overall integration rankings of the populations sampled from the nine Yugoslav regions are shown in Table 3, illustrating the range from the most highly integrated population (Bosnia-Hercegovina) to the least integrated (Kosmet).

TABLE 3

POLITICAL INTEGRATION RANKINGS OF YUGOSLAV POPULATIONS DEFINED ACCORDING TO CULTURE-REGION

Political Integration Ranking

Relatively More Integrated[a]	Threshold Level	Relatively Less Integrated
Bosnia-Hercegovina	Serbia Proper	Slovenia
Croatia-Slavonia		Adriatic Coast
Vojvodina		Macedonia
		Montenegro
		Kosmet

a. It should be noted that within each category, populations are ranked from high to low. That is, within the "more integrated" category, the population from Bosnia-Hercegovina ranks highest and that from the Vojvodina lowest. The same procedure will apply in all tables that follow.

The most obvious and striking feature concerning the rankings is the fact that those regions ranked as relatively "more integrated" and at the threshold level are centrally located in Yugoslavia (the heartland), while those ranked as relatively less integrated are the regions located on the geographic periphery of the country. Slovenia, Macedonia, Montenegro, Kosmet, and the Adriatic Coast are with no exceptions the *most removed from the center of the country and the capital in Belgrade,* and all rank least integrated on the Political Integration Index (see Figure 2).

The rankings derived from the index imply that the mountainous heartland and the peripheral zones present critical implications in terms of attitudes toward the formation of a unified federal state. The data indicate that orientations expressed in Montenegro or Macedonia relating to a sense of political community are significantly different (i.e., less integrated) than the orientations expressed in Croatia-Slavonia. Overall, it is quite clear that those populations coming from the peripheral zones are less inclined to

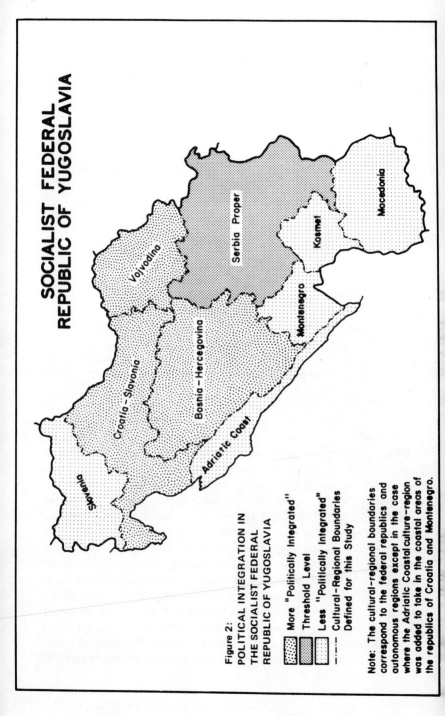

SOCIALIST FEDERAL
REPUBLIC OF YUGOSLAVIA

Figure 2:
POLITICAL INTEGRATION IN
THE SOCIALIST FEDERAL
REPUBLIC OF YUGOSLAVIA

More "Politically Integrated"
Threshold Level
Less "Politically Integrated"
Cultural-Regional Boundaries
Defined for this Study

Note: The cultural-regional boundaries
correspond to the federal republics and
autonomous regions except in the case
where the Adriatic Coastal culture-region
was added to take in the coastal areas of
the republics of Croatia and Montenegro.

break or loosen ties with more parochial particularistic elements within the Yugoslav context.

On the basis of other research the author would be led to suggest that as the barriers created by Yugoslavia's geographical features diminish, as a result of increasingly modernized communication and transit systems, the ability and propensity for Yugoslavia's peripheral zones to become more integrated will increase.[10] For purposes of the analysis herein, however, we only mean to draw attention to the fact that where a Yuogslav lives is closely related to his attitudes on the Political Integration Index. In other words, there appear to be serious "integrative repercussions" relating to the peripheral zone's isolation from the political centers of the society. The Yugoslav government has indicated, however, that possibilities do exist and efforts are being made to integrate the more southern peripheral areas. The Yugoslav economic policy of investing more aid in the backward outlying areas (although decreased somewhat since the economic reforms of 1965) has had a possible effect of increasing their sense of identification and community in relation to the federal system. This same economic policy, however, while representing an attempt to integrate the underdeveloped southern zones, has been a major cause of cleavage between the developed and underdeveloped areas. While perhaps having the propensity to integrate the southern zones, it may be causing the more modernized regions (e.g., Slovenia) to view the backward peripheral regions with self-interested skepticism and thereby impede the overall integration process.

When shifting to focus on specific culture-regional populations, some interesting findings develop. Table 4 gives the number of more integrated and less integrated scores as well as the integration ranking for each population. When viewing these scores it is evident that Bosnia-Hercegovina, Croatia-Slavonia, and Vojvodina rank as considerably more integrated than all other populations. It is interesting to note that Bosnia-Hercegovina ranks as very highly integrated despite its internal ethnic and religious complexity. Its heterogeneous ethnic composition is reflected in our sample whereby 50% of the population drawn from Bosnia-Hercegovina declared themselves as Serb, 11% as Croats, and 29% as Moslems, with the other 10% divided among Slovenes, Montenegrins, Hungarians, and Yugoslavians. The ethnic mix of Serbs, Croats, and Moslems, along with the heterogeneous religious environment (our sample reflected 49% Athiest, 17% Orthodox, 4% Catholic, and 25% Moslem) may in fact establish a setting conducive to political integration. It is sufficiently clear, however, that no other culture-region is characterized by the mixing of nationality and religious elements to the extent of

TABLE 4

SCORES OF CULTURE-REGION POPULATIONS
ON THE POLITICAL INTEGRATION INDEX

Culture-Regions	Integration Ranking	Integration Scores on Evaluative Statements	
		More Integrated	Less Integrated
Bosnia-Hercegovina	+7	+7	0
Croatia-Slavonia	+5	+6	−1
Vojvodina	+4	+7	−3
Serbia Proper	0	+3	−3
Slovenia	−2	+4	−6
Adriatic Coast	−2	+2	−4
Macedonia	−3	+3	−6
Montenegro	−3	+3	−6
Kosmet	−5	+2	−7

Bosnia-Hercegovina, and also, no other region is characterized by the extremely high level of political integration.

The findings suggest that the environment present in a region of ethnic and religious complexity may have an effect on the amelioration and minimization of national differences while furthering a federal or multinational orientation. As an indication of this effect, we find that within the extremely complex Bosnian culture-region, only 27.8% of the population agreed with the statement in the Political Integration Index contending that: "Nationality is important in our country." The response of the population from the Slovenian culture-region with its very homogeneous ethnic (sample reflected 98% Slovene) and religious composition, showed 71.9% in agreement with the same statement.

Croatia-Slavonia also ranks relatively high on the Political Integration Index. The only dimension on which it fails to receive a more integrated score is that reflected in the statement concerning "a willingness to move within Yugoslavia if one finds better work in other areas." Serbia Proper, on the other hand, ranks comparatively low when taking into consideration her central location and dominant position in present-day Yugoslavia.

A possible explanation of Slovenia's relatively low integration ranking has to take into account her present relationship to the rest of Yugoslavia. As noted earlier, Slovenia is by far the most homogeneous culture-region and economically developed zone in the federal republic. Our sample of the region reveals, for example, that 100% of the Slovenians were drawn from what our coding classified as developed environs and that 98%

considered themselves of Slovene ethnicity. This ethnic homogeneity, along with a high level of economic development, may place the Slovenian population in a position of relative psychological independence from the larger Yugoslav community. Slovenia's continued opposition to subsidization programs aiding the underdeveloped regions is probably indicative and additional evidence of the region's stance toward the greater Yugoslav state. Accordingly, if such a federal state means slowing down economic development in Slovenia, then the low Slovenian ranking on the integration index can be interpreted as a logical response and reflection of her own regional self-interests.

When considering the regional populations from the south, we find that the populations from Macedonia, Montenegro, and Kosmet all reflect very low integration rankings. All three of these southern populations rank less integrated and receive minus scores on the statements concerning "speaking one's own dialect," "the importance of nationality," and "speaking with the opposition." The responses to these statements clearly reflect an inability on the part the populations in these regions to loosen or sever ties with more parochial particularistic interests. An explanation of this inability may be accounted for by viewing separately the geographical-cultural environments characterizing Macedonia and Kosmet and also the unique Montenegrin setting. First, Macedonia is, in political terms, a recent addition to the Yugoslav state. Although given republic status in the post World War II federal system, the temporal opportunity to modify more particularistic belief systems has been minimal. And although Kosmet, with its predominant Albanian population, now enjoys the status of an autonomous province (and would like very much to see it raised to republic status), it is still the least mobilized and most parochial of all Yugoslav populations and can be expected to continue lagging in regard to the integration component.

The population from Montenegro is also characterized by geographical, socioeconomic, and cultural conditions that may encourage particularistic parochial interests and hinder an overriding sense of "Yugoslavism." The Montenegrins are isolated from much of the rest of Yugoslavia by harsh and rugged mountainlands. An obvious result is that the traditional Montenegrin character is more closely tied to parochial interests, and as a result, more integrative interests tend to suffer. At any rate, it is clear that the dominant influence of the geographical environment has left an indelible mark upon the integrative orientations of the Montenegrin population.

NATIONALITY

When considering populations as delineated on the basis of national identification, those claiming the nationality of Yugoslavian rank considerably "more integrated" than all other populations (see Table 5). Those claiming this nationality may represent potentially the embodiment of a new overriding "Yugoslav nationalism," in contrast to the traditional nationalism based on the various historical groups. In order to interpret the interesting ranking of the Yugoslavians it might be instructive to consider the social composition of the group. First, the data indicate that those claiming this nationality in our sample come from diverse cultural, regional backgrounds. The sample reflects 22% from Serbia Proper, 25% from Croatia-Slavonia, 14% from Bosnia-Hercegovina, 8% from Vojvodina, 17% from the Adriatic Coast, with the other 14% divided among the four remaining regions. Therefore, it is interesting to note that those individuals claiming a Yugoslavian nationality ranked as the most integrated group *even though they were drawn from every geographical area within the country.*

TABLE 5

POLITICAL INTEGRATION RANKINGS OF YUGOSLAV POPULATIONS DEFINED ACCORDING TO NATIONALITY

Political Integration Ranking

Relatively More Integrated	Threshold Level	Relatively Less Integrated
Yugoslavian	Hungarian	Slovene
	Serb	Montenegrin
	Croat	Macedonian
	Moslem	Albanian

Closer analysis makes it clear that the individual claiming a Yugoslavian nationality represents a unique citizen in that society. Our figures reveal that 81% of this population have completed at least a gymnasium or middle school education, 85% are under 45 years of age, 88% are Atheists, and 70% are Communists. These individuals may represent a new element within Yugoslav society, young and highly educated, with an overriding sense of Yugoslavism. Indicative of this orientation is the Yugoslavian response to the statement in the integration index, reading that: "It is important for a man to speak his own dialect." Whereas only 48% of the

Yugoslavians agreed with this statement, 91% of the Montenegrins and 100% of the Albanians agreed. Furthermore, whereas only 29% of the Yugoslavians agreed with the statement in the index reading that: "Nationality is important in our country," 74% of the Macedonians and 82% of the Albanians agreed. These examples are indicative of the multinational orientation of the Yugoslav population, an orientation which distinguishes them sharply from other segments of the greater population.

Table 6 illustrates that while no other nationality population scored higher than +2 on the integration index, the Yugoslavians received a +9. It will be interesting to follow the future growth or decline of those claiming the Yugoslavian nationality. If the number grows, the trend may be viewed as a "thaw" in the long-standing ethnic and religious hatreds that have characterized the South Slavs over the years. However, if the number of citizens claiming the nationality declines or remains static, ethnic and religious attachments will most likely remain preeminent and genuine integration into a multinational political community will suffer.

TABLE 6

**SCORES OF NATIONALITY POPULATIONS
ON THE POLITICAL INTEGRATION INDEX**

Nationality Populations	Integration Ranking	Integration Scores on Evaluative Statements	
		More Integrated	Less Integrated
Yugoslavian	+9	+9	0
Hungarian	+2	+6	−4
Serb	0	+3	−3
Croat	0	+3	−3
Moslem	−1	+3	−4
Slovene	−2	+4	−6
Montenegrin	−2	+4	−6
Macedonian	−3	+3	−6
Albanian	−5	+2	−7

The two major nationality populations, the Serbs and Croats along with the minority populations of Moslems and Hungarians, rank at the threshold level of integration. Their positions seem to reflect an orientation bordering on skepticism toward the "Yugoslav Idea." Although the Orthodox Serbs and the Catholic Croats may no longer be dominated totally by self-interested, ethnoreligious concerns, it appears that they are still not ready to dissolve such concerns in the interests of an integrated Yugoslav community. The pattern of their particularistic concerns is clear; the fact that the populations still tend to think of themselves first as Serbs and Croats, and only secondly as Yugoslavians is reflected in the data.

The integration levels of the populations coming from the southern-most regions of the country reflect the lowest level of integration attitudes. The Montenegrins, Macedonians, and Albanians all assume less integrated positions on the index. Examples are the statements showing all three populations overwhelmingly contending that it is "important for a man to speak his own dialect" and that "nationality is important" in Yugoslav society. If lower levels of political integration are in fact associated with lower levels of political pacification, compliance, and stability, as Ake contends, then these three minority populations may have definite repercussions upon the orderly channeling of inputs and outputs and the future performance of the Yugoslav system.

ATTITUDINAL CONSENSUS

Attitudinal consensus in Yugoslavia, as noted earlier, refers to the degree of similarity among the systems of attitudes held by different populations within Yugoslavia. The issue is essentially one of comparing various attitudes which, it is maintained, reflect different dimensions of a Yugoslav political culture. This investigation has made an assessment of where particular populations stand in relation to the mean Yugoslav orientation on seventeen of these different dimensions.[11] If all populations reflect attitudes very similar to the Yugoslav mean on the various dimensions, we will be able to say that attitudinal consensus in Yugoslavia is very high. However, if a number of populations are diverged from the mean expression, the degree of consensus will be more problematical.

It was also maintained earlier that a consideration of political culture must take into account the multidimensional character of the concept. There are many evaluative orientations that go into the system of beliefs, symbols, and values which establish the psychological character pervading the society and providing a setting in which political action takes place. Therefore, an average Yugoslav response has been established on each of the dimensions represented in the Attitudinal Consensus Index. It has been calculated by taking the relative weights of each of the nationality groups in Yugoslavia (as based on proportional population figures) and combining their orientations on each of the dimensions to arrive at an average Yugoslav orientation.[12] Therefore, each population has been assessed in reference to how similar it was to each average Yugoslav orientation, with each orientation contributing to its overall score evaluating the extent of attitudinal consensus. Those populations very similar to the average were determined to be relatively more attitudinally similar; those populations ranking very differently from the average were classified as attitudinally dissimilar; and those populations ranking somewhere between similarity and dissimilarity were assigned the threshold level.

CULTURE-REGION

Table 7 shows the range of culture-region populations ranked on the index from the most similar (Croatia-Slavonia) to the least similar (Slovenia). The most striking finding is the extremely low ranking of the population inhabiting the region of Slovenia. Not only is Slovenia one of the least politically integrated culture-regions, as noted in the preceding section, but it is also the most divergent in its aggregate attitude structure.

TABLE 7

ATTITUDINAL CONSENSUS RANKINGS OF THE CULTURE-REGION POPULATIONS

Attitudinal Consensus Ranking

Attitudinally Similar	Threshold Level	Attitudinally Dissimilar
Croatia-Slavonia	Montenegro	Macedonia
Bosnia-Hercegovina	Kosmet	Vojvodina
Serbia Proper		Slovenia
Adriatic Coast		

In other words, of all culture-region populations, Slovenia is the most diverged from the average Yugoslav political attitudes as represented by the seventeen statements making up the index, while at the same time, being one of the least disposed toward the integration of a larger Yugoslav community.

When considering the populations from the six major culture-regions, four rank as very similar to the Yugoslav average while two rank as relatively different. Croatia-Slavonia, Bosnia-Hercegovina, Serbia Proper, and the Adriatic Coast are classified at the attitudinally similar level. Slovenia and Macedonia, on the other hand, rank as attitudinally dissimilar. Once again, as in the case of political integration, indications of the presence of a heartland-periphery or heartland-north/south gap become apparent (see Figure 3). The northernmost region in Yugoslavia and the southern-most region clearly contain strikingly different populations in terms of the seventeen cultural orientations when compared to the other four more centrally located major regions.

It is interesting to note that while the Slovene and Macedonian culture-regions both rank similarly (i.e., attitudinally dissimilar), they are in addition very dissimilar from one another, as well as from the average Yugoslav expression. Whereas the population from Slovenia reflects a predominantly Westernized and more modernized system of beliefs and values, the Macedonian population reflects the effects of more traditional and perhaps Turkish influences. It is possible to view these two populations on opposite poles of a continuum with the other four major culture-region populations clustered around the center. That is, Slovenia could be viewed as attitudinally diverged on one end of the continuum due to her highly Westernized value system; Serbia Proper, Croatia-Slavonia, Bosnia-Hercegovina, and the Adriatic Coast might occupy the center of the continuum due to their intermediate position between Western and Eastern influences; while Macedonia could be seen as occupying the culturally diverged pole on the other end of the continuum due to her traditional Easternized value system (individual value analysis of Eastern-ized-Westernized statements relating to this idea will be discussed in the following section under nationality). This finding lends itself to the conception of a Yugoslav West and a Yugoslav East which is so often mentioned in analyses of Yugoslav society.

On the whole, the variation between the consensus levels of the culture-regions is distinct, reflecting the wide divergence of attitudes that exist in that country (see Table 8). While the mean orientation of the Croatia-Slavonian population ranked within a standard deviation unit of the Yugoslav average on sixteen of the cultural dimensions, the Slovenian population did so on only four. Furthermore, the divergent effect of the social compositions of the populations drawn from the more unique areas of Montenegro, Kosmet, and Vojvodina are distinctly reflected in their consensus rankings. The homogeneous population from Montenegro (sampled reflected 96% Montenegrin and 85% Atheist) certainly did not fail to register their deviance from the Yugoslav average. Also Kosmet with its predominantly Albanian population and Vojvodina with its distinct Hungarian representation exhibit their relative divergence from the average Yugoslav orientations.

The levels of attitudinal agreement within these three more specialized

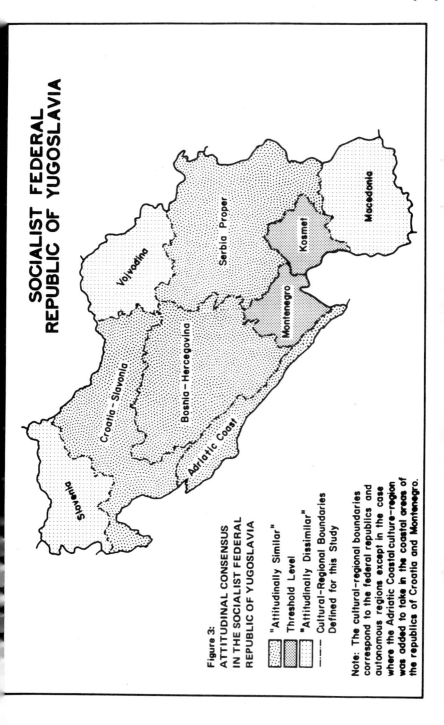

SOCIALIST FEDERAL REPUBLIC OF YUGOSLAVIA

Figure 3:
ATTITUDINAL CONSENSUS
IN THE SOCIALIST FEDERAL
REPUBLIC OF YUGOSLAVIA

"Attitudinally Similar"

Threshold Level

"Attitudinally Dissimilar"

Cultural-Regional Boundaries
Defined for this Study

Note: The cultural-regional boundaries
correspond to the federal republics and
autonomous regions except in the case
where the Adriatic Coastal culture-region
was added to take in the coastal areas of
the republics of Croatia and Montenegro.

TABLE 8

SCORES OF CULTURE-REGION POPULATIONS
ON THE ATTITUDINAL CONSENSUS INDEX

Culture Region	Consensus Ranking	Consensus Scores on Evaluative Statements	
		Attitudinally Similar	Attitudinally Dissimilar
Croatia-Slavonia	+15	+16	−1
Bosnia-Hercegovina	+13	+15	−2
Serbia Proper	+11	+14	−3
Adriatic Coast	+11	+14	−3
Montenegro	+ 5	+11	−6
Kosmet	+ 1	+ 9	−8
Macedonia	− 3	+ 7	−10
Vojvodina	− 3	+ 7	−10
Slovenia	− 9	+ 4	−13

culture-regions yield some interesting implications when compared with the four larger regions that have been classified as having greater similarity (see Table 9). The population from the three specialized regions, especially Vojvodina and Kosmet, reflect a comparatively high level of within-group solidarity in their attitudinal divergence from the Yugoslav average. Their average Leik consensus scores of .339 and .434 (−1.000 representing total dissensus and 1.000 total consensus) on the seventeen index statements are considerably higher than those of the more attitudinally similar populations.[13] Specifically, whereas all the culture-regional populations ranked as similar have average consensus scores below .200, all those populations not attaining this highest ranking have scores above .200. What this reflects is a relatively high level of agreement within the belief systems of the specialized divergent populations which have remained somewhat apart from the average Yugoslav expression. The continuum example cited earlier again lends itself to this finding. Those populations tending toward the two divergent poles are in higher internal agreement on the evaluative statements than are those clustering toward the center of the attitudinal continuum. This suggests that within the converged populations, what might be identified as pluralistic tendencies ensure that controversy is not lacking. In the contrasting dissimilar populations, on the other hand, agreement is rather high on the group's divergence and deviance from the Yugoslav average. This suggests that assimilation or movement of the divergent populations toward the center of the continuum (i.e., the

TABLE 9

AVERAGE WITHIN-POPULATION SCORES
ON THE STATEMENTS COMPRISING THE ATTITUDINAL
CONSENSUS INDEX FOR THE CULTURE-REGION POPULATIONS

Culture Regions	Average Leik Consensus Score on 17 Evaluative Statements
Attitudinally Similar	
Serbia Proper	.090
Adriatic Coast	.155
Bosnia-Hercegovina	.172
Croatia-Slavonia	.188
Threshold Level or Attitudinally Dissimilar	
Montenegro	.207
Macedonia	.241
Slovenia	.251
Vojvodina	.339
Kosmet	.434

Yugoslav average) will most likely be restricted because of the solidarity within the belief systems of these populations.

In summary, the consensus index clearly discriminates among the belief systems of the culture-regional populations. Four populations respond very similarly to the Yugoslav mean orientation on the seventeen evaluative statements, two populations respond in a relatively similar manner, and four populations respond differently. The responses of Kosmet, Macedonia, Vojvodina, and Slovenia indicate that if assimilation into a common culture and psychological inclusion into a common state is going to be an ideal of the multinational Yugoslav nation, then these four populations will have to make significant shifts within their respective belief systems.

NATIONALITY

When classifying populations according to nationality divisions, three populations fall in each of the three index categories (see Table 10). As noted earlier, the Serbs and Croats contribute more to a greater Yugoslav political culture than do the smaller nationality groups because of the size

TABLE 10

**ATTITUDINAL CONSENSUS RANKINGS OF THE
NATIONALITY POPULATIONS**

Attitudinal Consensus Ranking

Attitudinally Similar	Threshold Level	Attitudinally Dissimilar
Serb	Montenegrin	Macedonian
Croat	Yugoslavian	Slovene
Moslem	Albanian	Hungarian

factor, both in reality and in the statistical calculation using the survey data. It seems only logical for them to be more converged than some of the minority groups. The Slovene population, on the other hand, should also play a major role in determining the average Yugoslav orientation because of its comparatively large size. However, the data show that only the Hungarian population is more different from the Yugoslav mean orientation than is the Slovene (see Table 11). The Slovenes are in fact extremely far removed from the average political culture in present-day Yugoslavia and clearly show the effects of what can be identified as a more Westernized, modernized value system.

Once again the consensus continuum lends itself to an interpretation of the differing levels of attitudinal similarity. In that regard, the Serb and Croat populations may be viewed as occupying the midpoint (attitudinally similar), while the Slovene and Hungarian populations from the north may be seen as occupying one divergent pole and the Albanian and Macedonian populations from the south the other (see Figure 4). When selecting statements reflecting different dimensions of these so-called Westernized-Easternized attitudes, the suggestions derived from the convergence continuum are clarified and given further support. The Slovene population

Northern, Westernized Populations	Attitudinally Similar Populations	Southern, Easternized Populations
Slovene Hungarian Yugoslavian	Croat and Serb Moslem Montenegrin	Albanian Macedonian

Figure 4. NATIONALITY POPULATIONS RANKED ALONG A CONSENSUS CONTINUUM

TABLE 11

SCORES OF NATIONALITY POPULATIONS
ON THE ATTITUDINAL CONSENSUS INDEX

Nationality	Consensus Ranking	Consensus Scores on Evaluative Statements	
		Attitudinally Similar	Attitudinally Dissimilar
Serb	+17	+17	0
Croat	+17	+17	0
Moslem	+ 9	+13	4
Montenegrin	+ 3	+10	− 7
Yugoslavian	+ 1	+ 9	− 8
Albanian	+ 1	+ 9	− 8
Macedonian	− 3	+ 7	−10
Slovene	− 9	+ 4	−13
Hungarian	−11	+ 3	−14

consistantly reflects the more modern Westernized attitudes; the Serbs and Croats assume an intermediate position; and the Macedonians reflect the most traditional Easternized posture (see Table 12). It will be interesting to trace the movement of the specific populations over time on a continuum such as the one suggested in Figure 4. If the two poles are drawn increasingly closer to the center, one could realistically talk about increasingly attitudinal convergence, and perhaps by inference, cultural assimilation in Yugoslav society. If, however, the relative positioning of the populations remains static, then a comparatively high level of attitudinal and cultural divergence can be seen as continuing to characterize the system in the future.

It is also interesting to note that the Serbs and Croats may be no longer so bitterly and diametrically opposed as accounts of Yugoslav society have led us to believe. The data in Table 9 showed that both rank as attitudinally similar to the Yugoslav mean on all seventeen attitudinal dimensions. Some further interesting observations are evident when considering the seventeen responses in more depth. The statistical measures presented in Table 13 reveal any possible similarities or differences on the statements in terms of the typicality of responses (mean scores) between the Serb, Croat, and Slovene populations and also the level of agreement within each of these populations. It becomes suprisingly clear that the Serbs and Croats assume almost identical positions on each

TABLE 12

NATIONALITY POPULATION'S AGREEMENT WITH STATEMENTS REFLECTING MODERNIZED-TRADITIONAL AND WESTERNIZED-EASTERNIZED VALUES

Evaluative Statements	Percentage Answering in Agreement		
	Slovenes	Croats and Serbs	Macedonians
It is not necessary to talk with individuals whose thoughts are in opposition to ours.	3.1	22.3	34.3
The world always changes for the better.	52.0	78.3	90.5
Since all individuals have the same needs, differences in rewards should be minimal.	46.7	67.5	77.4
Individuals must be rewarded above all in accordance with the social significance of the work they perform.	47.4	58.7	72.4
The most important thing for children to learn is to obey their parents.	54.8	66.8	84.6

a. Interpretation: The higher the percentage of the population in agreement, the more traditional and Easternized the population.

of the statements both in terms of mean scores and in terms of the levels of agreement as represented by the Leik consensus score in each group. This finding would seem to imply that there is in fact a great deal of common ground between these two major populations upon which a greater Yugoslav political culture could be constructed. This fact would seem to present significant and encouraging implications in terms of the future political culture of the Yugoslav state. It seems apparent that if the two major, and heretofore, supposedly always contrasting and conflicting nationalities could be seen as representing a broad basis of cultural and attitudinal similarity rather than divergence, the myth of incompatibility could be broken down and psychological inclusion into a common state could be enhanced.

TABLE 13

MEAN SCORES AND CONSENSUS SCORES OF SERB, CROAT, AND SLOVENE
POPULATIONS ON THE SEVENTEEN EVALUATIVE STATEMENTS

		Mean and Consensus Scores on the Seventeen Statements Comprising the Attitudinal Consensus Index								
		1	2	3	4	5	6	7	8	9
Serb	CS[a]	.06	−.16	.03	.64	.21	.20	.32	.30	.02
	MS	1.94	2.53	2.26	1.36	2.34	3.21	2.13	1.70	2.37
Croat	CS	.05	−.24	.08	.55	.32	.13	.41	.35	.15
	MS	1.99	2.47	2.27	1.45	2.10	3.13	2.23	1.86	2.27
Slovene	CS	−.14	.10	.02	.40	.40	.75	.31	.22	.08
	MS	2.43	1.90	2.41	1.78	2.26	3.75	2.56	2.25	2.13

		10	11	13	13	14	15	16	17
Serb	CS	−.22	.06	.15	.28	−.01	.05	.20	.11
	MS	2.47	2.21	2.32	3.28	2.52	2.34	2.16	2.32
Croat	CS	−.05	.05	.09	.13	.04	.10	.19	.12
	MS	2.48	2.48	2.37	3.13	2.61	2.17	2.27	2.47
Slovene	CS	.20	.22	.24	.58	.20	.03	.08	.43
	MS	2.85	2.73	2.57	3.58	2.72	2.55	2.59	3.43

a. CS denotes the Leik Consensus Score and MS denotes the Mean Score for the respective populations.

When comparing the response configurations of the Slovenes to that of the Serbs and Croats, however, we find one of the distinct cleavages that exists within Yugoslav society. Whereas the average responses of the two major groups were very similar to one another, the average Slovene responses show considerable dissimilarity to those of the other two populations. This again reflects the divergence of the Slovene population and illustrates that the Croats are attitudinally closer to the Serbs as reflected in these seventeen dimensions.

Closer analysis of all 38 attitudinal statements included in the questionnaire identifies this attitudinal cleavage in even greater clarity. By using correlation analysis and tests of statistical significance, the data indicate distinctly the lines of attitudinal similarity and dissimilarity existing between the various nationality populations. When that mode of analysis is applied to all 38 attitudinal statements included in the survey instrument, we find the following differences between the four largest Yugoslav populations (Croat, Serb, Slovene, and Macedonian) at the .01 level of statistical significance:

(1) statistically significant differences exist between the Serbs and Croats on only 3 statements with very low measures of association

(2) significant differences exist between the Serb-Croats (combined) and the Slovene on 23 statements with high measures of association

(3) significant differences exist between the Serb-Croats and Macedonians on 18 statements with high measures of association

(4) significant differences exist between the Slovenes and Macedonians on 25 statements with extremely high measures of association

This finding follows closely with the consensus continuum discussed earlier. While there are almost no attitudinal differences between the similar populations (i.e., Serbs and Croats), there is considerable difference between them and the populations on the divergent ends of the continuum (i.e., Slovenes and Macedonians). And most striking, there is extreme attitudinal cleavage between the two divergent populations. Or stated differently, differences are evident between the Westernized populations and the intermediate populations, and the intermediate populations and the Easternized populations; however, the striking differences and the deepest cleavage exist between the Westernized and Easternized (or north and south) populations as illustrated by the continuum (see Figure 5).

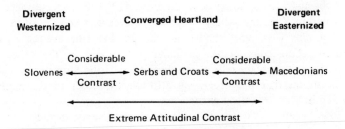

Figure 5. **NATIONALITY POPULATIONS RANKED ALONG THE CONSENSUS CONTINUUM**

When focusing upon the intriguing Yugoslavian nationality population, it is interesting to note that while they were very favorably oriented toward the integration of a unified Yugoslav community, they are only at the threshold level with respect to attitudinal consensus (see Tables 10 and 11). This is of course rather logical; a reexamination of the integration index shows that the Yugoslavians are quite different (i.e., attitudinally dissimilar) in relation to other populations as is reflected in the six dimensions; i.e., they were far more politically integrated than the other groups. Accordingly, on eight of the seventeen statements making up the consensus index, the Yugoslavians received minus scores for being outside the level judged similar to the total sample's orientation. On many of these statements the Yugoslavians reflected more modernized, liberal, and progressive values than did the greater population. As a result, their consensus level was relatively low.

This is again a validation of the contention made at the outset of this analysis, i.e., that different populations will occupy different positions along the roads to political integration and attitudinal consensus in a dynamic developing social system. The position on the two indices of those claiming a Yugoslavian nationality is indicative of this contention. The Yugoslavians are far ahead of the other populations in reference to the integration process, and, as a result, are quite different from most of the populations in reference to the consensus component. The very fact that they are so markedly ahead in integration makes them dissimilar from the average Yugoslav posture; therefore, they rank no higher than at the threshold level on the consensus index.

CONCLUSION

The primary concern of this paper has been the exploration of two central components of the nation-building process in Yugoslav society. It has been maintained that by exploring the components of political integration and attitudinal consensus through the use of survey data, a reflection of the current character of various diverse populations within Yugoslavia could be afforded. Furthermore, it was contended that within a constantly evolving system such as that of Yugoslavia, an assessment of the relative posture of such populations is of intrinsic importance if one intends to gain an understanding of the belief systems encouraging integration and assimilation, as well as the systems that engender their counterparts, disintegration and divergence. Both types of configurations were found to be present in Yugoslavia and both present critical implications in terms of the future evolution of the Yugoslav state.

The investigation has attempted to avoid making unwarranted or misleading speculations about the effects of different levels of integration and consensus on the future functioning of the system; e.g., that Yuogslavia's developmental prospects are unavoidably pessimistic unless rapid paces of integration and attitudinal convergence are achieved. For it may be that the dynamic evolution of the system thrives on certain levels of disintegrative orientations and divergent belief systems. However, the majority of the literature addressing itself to this question is based upon the contention and assumption that higher levels of political integration and attitudinal agreement are associated with higher levels of political pacification, compliance, and stability. Therefore, if a political scientist, policy maker, or social engineer places value upon such characteristics within a political system, the concepts investigated within this chapter should be viewed as relevant and important aspects affecting the evolution of any society.

It should be noted in conclusion that the Political Integration Index distinguished between Yugoslav populations that held orientations conducive to increasing a relationship of community within the larger political entity and those populations that did not. In that regard, the populations drawn from the heartland regions of Bosnia-Hercegovina and Croatia-Slavonia were characterized as possessing orientations most conducive to the development of a larger Yugoslav community, or, in other words, were more politically integrated than any other culture-regional populations. When using the nationality breakdown, those claiming to be Yugoslavians were considerably more integrated than any other nationality population, suggesting the possibilities of a new, more federally oriented Yugoslav character. Furthermore, even though the Serb and Croat nationalities ranked relatively high (threshold level) on the integration index, the presence of skeptical or somewhat anti-integrative orientations toward a more unified Yugoslav state were definitely present.

The Slovenian population, defined both on the basis of culture-region and nationality (and in this instance they are almost identical populations) assumed a particularly interesting position. Their collective responses indicated that they were least willing to be integrated into the greater Yugoslav state. Along with the Macedonians, they rank lower on the integration index than do any other major culture-region or nationality populations. The low rankings of the populations from Slovenia and Macedonia, along with those from the Adriatic Coast, Montenegro, and Kosmet, suggested strikingly the presence of a heartland-periphery division in Yugoslavia. Without exception, the populations occupying the heartland regions were characterized as more highly integrated, while those from the peripheral zones were likely to be less integrated. This heartland-periphery gap reflects one of the dominant cleavage systems effecting the integration and nation-building process in present-day Yugoslavia.

The Attitudinal Consensus Index provided a useful instrument for determining where particular populations stood in relation to the average Yugoslav orientation as reflected by the seventeen evaluative statements included in the index. The major culture-regions of Croatia-Slavonia, Bosnia-Hercegovina, Serbia Proper, and the Adriatic Coast, and also the Serb and Croat nationality populations proved to be most converged or similar to a mean Yugoslav orientation. Slovenia and Macedonia, as in the Political Integration Index, exhibited belief systems considerably different from the average Yugoslav expression. Once again, the presence of cleavage within Yugoslav society along geographical boundaries was clear. The data indicated that the divergent north and divergent south remain attitudinally dissimilar from the more centrally located regions in Yugoslavia. Furthermore, consensus scores revealed a comparatively high level of agreement within these populations. Such solidarity within these populations will undoubtably present rather deep-rooted barriers to efforts promoting unity or convergence across population boundaries.

The Attitudinal Consensus Index also showed some surprising similarities between populations that in the past have been thought to be widely divergent and in extreme cultural conflict. The Serb and Croat populations reflected interesting similarities in their attitudinal configurations both in terms of their typical or average responses and their levels of agreement on these responses. On the other hand, the divergent northern and southern populations showed considerable dissimilarity from the heartland populations, and also exhibited extreme divergency from one another. Therefore, the data have shown the extreme differences in political orientations to be more critical in the heartland-periphery, north-south, or modernized-traditional gap, than in the most often cited Serb-Croat cleavage. Identification of such lines of attitudinal cleavage seems of critical importance in order to either verify or dispose of some of the perhaps impressionistic myths that have been prevalent in reference to the nation-building process in that country.

When combining the two components of the process, some definite implications about the future of the multinational state become clear (see Tables 14 and 15). As noted earlier, populations ranking high on both components can be assumed to be most favorably oriented toward the Yugoslav multinational experiment (e.g., the populations from Croatia-Slavonia and Bosnia-Hercegovina), while populations ranking low on both components (e.g., Macedonians and Slovenians) can be seen as least favorably oriented in reference to the nation-building process. Therefore, the data clearly illustrate that the populations from Croatia-Slavonia and Bosnia-Hercegovina are the most favorably disposed toward the establishment of a multinational community, and most similar to what has been defined and evaluated as the average Yugoslav expression on seventeen cultural orientations. These groups, it is reasonable to maintain, will contribute most to the coherence and predictability of political life in the multinational Yugoslav context. The populations from the most northern and southern regions of the country, however, illustrate contrasting belief systems and present different and probably less favorable political implications from the Yugoslav point of view. These two groups, the Slovenes and the Macedonians, are least integrated and least converged of all Yugoslav populations. Their dispositions are such as to encourage cultural particularism rather than a sense of multinational unity. Furthermore, the cultural orientations of these two peripheral populations are very dissimilar from an average Yugoslav expression. The Slovenes in the north represent a predominantly modernized Westernized belief system while the Macedonians in the south represent a more traditional Turkicized perspective. In short, they are neither favorably disposed toward the miltinational experiment, nor similar to an average Yugoslav expression. Identification and support have not been transferred from more parochial regional and ethnic interests to the multinational system of which they are members.

TABLE 14

**TYPOLOGY CLASSIFYING CULTURE-REGION POPULATIONS
AS THEY RELATE TO THE NATION-BUILDING PROCESS**

Attitudinal Consensus

		High	Medium	Low
	High	Croatia-Slavonia Bosnia-Hercegovina		Vojvodina
Political Integration	Medium	Serbia Proper		
	Low	Adriatic Coast	Montenegro Kosmet	Macedonia Slovenia

TABLE 15

TYPOLOGY CLASSIFYING NATIONALITY POPULATIONS
AS THEY RELATE TO THE NATION-BUILDING PROCESS

Attitudinal Consensus

		High	Medium	Low
	High		Yugoslavian	
Political Integration	Medium	Serb Croat Moslem		Hungarian
	Low		Montenegrin Albanian	Macedonian Slovene

Those populations ranking high in terms of one component and low in terms of the other also hold interesting positions along the potential paths leading to a more highly integrated and converged state (see Table 14). For example, Vojvodina's classification on the culture-region typology implies that the population residing within her boundaries is favorably oriented toward the attitudinal preconditions of a larger Yugoslav community, but at the same time remains attitudinally diverged in relation to the average Yugoslav population. The Vojvodinan population's high political integration ranking could be a result of her geographical proximity and accessibility to the Yugoslav political center (Belgrade). On the other hand, her low consensus ranking can be traced to a cultural heritage that is clearly divergent from the majority of the Yugoslav peoples.

The individuals inhabiting the Adriatic Coastal region reflect the opposite characteristics (see Table 14). Their low integration ranking may illustrate their geographical and psychological isolation from the federal political structures, while their high convergence ranking could reflect their close ties to the greater Yugoslav heritage and cultural tradition. These two examples illustrate the utility and importance of assessing populations in terms of both components. By doing so, one can make a more complete and, hopefully, more valid assessment of the relative postures of the different populations in contemporary Yugoslavia. In short, in order to fully understand movement toward or away from political integration and attitudinal consensus, and the nation-building process in general, one must first know where different segments of the population stand.

Although this analysis has attempted exactly that, considerable research remains to be carried out focusing upon the causes and consequences of the components investigated in this study. More detailed research should pursue these challenges by attempting to isolate the relevant factors related to changes in levels of integration and consensus. Then, attempts must be made to link these two components to various characteristics (e.g., political stability) of the developing nation. It is hoped that such efforts, as well as the one included herein, will move us closer to an adequate theory of nation-building and a more plausible explanation of the growth and decline of political communities.

APPENDIX A: THE INVENTORIES

Inventory I

Evaluative Statements Comprising Political Integration Index and Interpretations of the Respective Statements (Responses to Each Statement coded: 1–Strongly Agree, 2–Agree, 3–Disagree, 4–Strongly Disagree).

1. "It is important for a man to speak his own dialect."

   Interpretation: Since language and dialect have been a major divisive force through South Slavic history, agreement with the statement exhibits an element of particularism within the Yugoslav context; therefore, the higher the level of agreement, the *lower* the level of political integration.

2. "Nationality is important in our country."

   Interpretation: Since nationality is perhaps the single most divisive element within Yugoslav society today, agreement with the statement reflects a form of national particularism; therefore, the higher the level of agreement, the *lower* the level of political integration.

3. "A man must settle in another region of Yugoslavia if he finds better work there."

   Interpretation: Since one aspect of national-regional particularism has been an unwillingness to move and inhabit other culturally different areas, agreement with the statement shows a tolerance and acceptance toward other areas; therefore, the higher the level of agreement, the *higher* the level of political integration.

4. "State celebrations (i.e., Yugoslav) are important for me."

   Interpretation: Since Yugoslav state holidays and celebrations are often slighted and the national counterparts emphasized, agreement with the statement expresses a form of countrywide, Yugoslav patriotism; therefore, higher agreement represents *higher* integration levels.

5. "A man can have faith in the majority of the (Yugoslav) people."

   Interpretation: Since traditional domestic relations among the South Slavs have encouraged distrust among the various ethnic and religious groups, agreement with the statement shows a relative absence of this feeling; therefore, *higher* agreement represents higher integration levels.

6. "It is not necessary to talk with individuals whose thoughts are in opposition to ours."

   Interpretation: Since agreement with the question shows an unwillingness to communicate and an intolerance for the diversity of thought that exists in Yugoslavia, the higher the level of agreement, the *lower* the level of political integration.

Inventory II

Evaluative Statements Comprising Cultural Convergence Index (Responses coded: 1–Strongly Agree, 2–Agree, 3–Disagree, 4–Strongly Disagree).

1. It is important for a man to speak his own dialect.
2. Nationality is important in our country.
3. A man must settle in another region of Yugoslavia if he finds better work there.
4. State celebrations (i.e., Yugoslav) are important to me.
5. A man can have faith in the majority of the (Yugoslav) people.
6. It is not necessary to talk with individuals whose thoughts are in opposition to ours.
7. Voters meetings contribute to fulfilling the will of the working people.
8. The world always changes for the better.
9. Human nature is such that there will always be war and conflict.
10. In order to fulfill their personal goals and personal desires individuals must compete with and subdue one another.
11. It is better to change society by rapid, planned means than by a gradual, natural path.
12. The price of a television set depends upon the number of televisions on the market.
13. A table on which a tablemaker works for ten days, is worth more than the same kind of table that the same tablemaker made in five days.

14. A rapid pace of economic development depends heavily on a strong centralized authority.

15. Since all individuals have the same needs, differences in rewards should be minimal.

16. Individuals must be rewarded above all in accordance with the social significance of the work they perform.

17. When self-administration is achieved there will no longer be conflicts and problems in our society.

APPENDIX B: THE INDEXES

I. Constructing the Political Integration Index:

Six evaluative statements were selected from a total list of 38 structured response statements included in the questionnaire. Each statement was judged as representing one of the specific dimensions of political integration discussed fully within the body of the paper. Mean scores were initially calculated on each of the statements for the entire Yugoslav sample. This mean score was taken as the point to be used as a basis for comparison to specific populations within the total sample.

The mean score, for example, for the total sample on statement 1 ("It is important for a man to speak his own dialect.") was 1.97. If the mean score of a specific population within the total sample was higher than 1.97 (and thus was in higher disagreement with statement 1), then it received a plus (+) 1 or plus (+) 2 for being "more integrated" than the average Yugoslav orientation. If the population's mean score was higher than the average Yugoslav mean score, but less than 1 standard deviation divided by 4 higher, it received a plus 1. However, if the population's mean score was more than 1 standard deviation divided by 4 higher than the Yugoslav mean, it received a plus 2. If the population's mean score was lower than that of the average Yugoslav score, it was assigned a minus (−) 1 or minus (−) 2. It received a minus 1 if it was lower but less than 1 standard deviation divided by 4 lower, and a minus 2 if it was lower and outside of the standard deviation unit. Therefore, the range of scores can be from +12 to −12.

Then, population's "more integrated" scores were compared with its "less integrated" scores with the difference being applied to the ranking index in order to obtain a political integration ranking for each population. It should be noted that these rankings are only relative rather than absolute values. That is, population A should not be called "integrated," but only "more integrated" than population B.

II. Constructing the Attitudinal Consensus Index:

Seventeen evaluative statements were selected from the questionnaire to construct the Attitudinal Consensus Index. Each statement was judged as representing an attitudinal orientation that reflected the Yugoslav system of beliefs, symbols, and values which defines the situation in which political action takes place; i.e., the statements were selected as orientations representing dimensions of Yugoslav political culture. The index purports to measure how similar various populations (defined according to culture-region and nationality) are to the average Yugoslav orientation on each of the evaluative statements.

Mean scores were initially calculated on each of the seventeen statements for the entire Yugoslav sample. Mean scores were calculated also for each of the defined populations within the total sample in order to assess how similar the specific populations were in relation to the average Yugoslav score. In order to establish a base point which would permit assessment of the relative distance of each population from the Yugoslav mean, a standard deviation was calculated for the entire population on each evaluative statement.

This standard deviation was then divided by four in order to be of use in the following way: If the mean score of a specific population fell inside of 1 standard deviation divided by 4 of the Yugoslav mean, then it received a score of plus (+) 1 (Attitudinally Similar) for that statement. If its mean score fell outside of 1 standard deviation divided by 4, then it received a score of minus (−) 1 (Attitudinally Dissimilar) for that statement. Therefore, each population had the possibility of receiving seventeen +'s (Attitudinally Similar Scores), seventeen −'s (Attitudinally Dissimilar Scores), or any combination of the two scores. A population's Attitudinally Similar Scores were compared with its Attitudinally Dissimilar Scores with the difference then being applied to the index in order to obtain a ranking for each population. Again, it should be noted that the ranking establishes a relative rather than an absolute value.

III. Statistical Note on the Leik Consensus Score

The Leik Consensus Score is derived from a test based on cumulative relative frequency using ordinal data. The score can range from −1 (complete dissensus with responses evenly divided on opposite ends of the response continuum) to +1 (complete consensus, with all responses in one response category). Responses divided evenly in each of the response categories would yield a score of 0. (For a complete description of the statistic, see Leik, 1966: 85-90).

APPENDIX C: THE POLITICAL INTEGRATION AND ATTITUDINAL CONSENSUS INDEXES

I. Political Integration Index

A. Procedures Used in Assigning Political Integration Rankings

Integration Scores on Evaluative Statements	Political Integration Ranking
+4 to +9	Relatively More Integrated
+3 to −1	Threshold Level
−2 to −5	Relatively Less Integrated

B. Political Integration Rankings of Culture-Region and Nationality Populations

Political Integration Ranking

	Relatively More Integrated	Threshold Level	Relatively Less Integrated
Culture-Regions	Bosnia-Hercegovina Croatia-Slavonia Vojvodina	Serbia Proper	Slovenia Adriatic Coast Macedonia Montenegro Kosmet
Nationalities	Yugoslavian	Hungarian Serb Croat Moslem	Slovene Montenegrin Macedonian Albanian

II. Attitudinal Consensus Index

A. Procedures Used in Assigning Rankings

Consensus Scores on Evaluative Statements	Attitudinal Consensus Ranking
+7 to +15	Attitudinally Similar
+6 to −2	Threshold Level
−3 to −11	Attitudinally Dissimilar

B. Attitudinal Consensus Rankings of Culture-Region and Nationality Populations

Attitudinal Consensus Ranking

	Attitudinally Similar	Threshold Level	Attitudinally Dissimilar
Culture-Regions	Croatia-Slavonia Bosnia-Hercegovina Serbia proper Adriatic Coast	Montenegro Kosmet	Macedonia Vojvodina Slovenia
Nationalities	Serb Croat Moslem	Montenegrin Yugoslavian Albanian	Macedonian Slovene Hungarian

NOTES

1. It may be somewhat misleading to use the term "nation-building" within the multinational Yugoslav environment. However, since the term "nation-state" is used most often to identify the new South Slavic union, the term nation-building will be used as a matter of convenience to refer to the phenomena surrounding the construction of the new (i.e., post-World War II) Yugoslav state.

2. Consult Appendix A, I, for a complete listing of the evaluative statements and interpretations comprising the Political Integration Index.

3. The techniques of index construction are discussed in a later section entitled "Measurement Techniques."

4. Consult Appendix A, II, for a complete listing of the evaluative statements comprising the Attitudinal Consensus Index. Note this index includes the items composing the Political Integration Index as well as eleven additional evaluative statements drawn from the questionnaire. We can justify the presence of the integration items in both indices because the items shall be used rather differently in each case. In the integration index, the content of one's response is of central importance (i.e., the degree of integration), whereas in the consensus index, only the extent of divergence from the greater Yugoslav attitudinal average is of relevance.

5. In regard to the interpretation distinguishing between a more integrated and less integrated score, the reader is asked again to refer to Appendix A, I.

6. Consult Appendix B, I, for a complete explanation of the methods used in assigning the integration rankings.

7. It should be apparent that this is a different procedure than that used for the Political Integration Index. Again, it should be stressed that in the former, it was important to know whether a population's mean score fell above or below the Yugoslav mean score. In this case it makes no difference; only the absolute distance (i.e., the extent of divergence) from the average Yugoslav mean (either above or below) affects the population's consensus score.

8. Consult Appendix B, II, for a complete explanation of the methods used in assigning the consensus rankings.

9. The reader should be reminded that the term nationalism as used in the Yugoslav context means nationalism of individual nations and nationality groups such as Croatian and Serbian, rather than a Yugoslav or South Slav nationalism.

10. The author's dissertation research has shown that as Yugoslav populations become more mobilized (based upon a Deutsch-type index of social mobilization), they become more modern and less particularistic in their beliefs (see, e.g., Bertsch, 1970).

11. It may be useful once again to consult Appendix B, II, for a detailed discussion of the Attitudinal Consensus Index.

12. In effect, this means that since Yugoslavia is made up of 40% Serbs and 5% Macedonians, Serbs will have eight times the weight or influence of Macedonians in determining an empirically based average Yugoslav orientation. Or, stated differently, if every individual's orientation were averaged in order to arrive at a Yugoslav orientation, Serbs would have eight times the influence in determining that orientation. This was determined to be the most reasonable strategy for assessing the relative importance of both majority and minority nationalities in establishing average Yugoslav orientations. Fortunately, our sample closely reflected the

nationality composition of the country, so no major statistical manipulation was required.

13. See Appendix B, III, for more detailed explanations of the Leik consensus measure. Also see Leik, 1966.

REFERENCES

AKE, C. (1967) A Theory of Political Integration. Homewood, Ill.: Dorsey.

BERTSCH, G. K. (1970) "Community-building and the Individual in Yugoslav Society." Ph.D. dissertation. University of Oregon.

DEUTSCH, K. and W. J. FOLTZ [ed.] (1963) Nation-Building. New York: Atherton.

HOFFMAN, G. W. and F. W. NEAL (1962) Yugoslavia and the New Communism. New York: Twentieth Century Fund.

KERNER, R. J. (1949) Yugoslavia. Berkeley, Calif.: Univ. of California Press.

LEIK, R. (1966) "A measure of ordinal consensus." Pacific Soc. Rev. 9 (Fall).

PYE, L. and S. VERBA [eds.] (1965) Political Culture and Political Development. Princeton, N.J.: Princeton Univ. Press.

SHOUP, P. (1968) Communism and the Yugoslav National Question. New York: Columbia Univ. Press.

ZANINOVICH, M. G. (1968) The Development of Socialist Yugoslavia. Baltimore: John Hopkins Press.

GARY K. BERTSCH is Assistant Professor and Director of Undergraduate Studies at the University of Georgia. During the year 1969-70, he was International Research and Exchanges Board Exchange Professor in Zagreb (Yugoslavia) where he was attached to the Faculty of Political Science and conducted research focusing upon various aspects of Yugoslav political development and societal integration. He has co-authored (with M. George Zaninovich) the forthcoming book Yugoslavia: Patterns of Cleavage in the Quest for Community. *He is currently working on the design of a five-nation study of industrialization and social-psychological change.*